unity   W9-BYJ-176

What Do LIBRARIANS Do?

Mary Austen

PowerKiDS press.

New York

Published in 2016 by The Rosen Publishing Group, Inc.
29 East 21st Street, New York, NY 10010

First Edition

Editor: Katie Kawa
Book Design: Katelyn Heinle

Photo Credits: Cover (librarian), pp. 1, 13 Mark Edward Atkinson/Blend Images/Getty Images; cover (hands) bymandesigns/Shutterstock.com; back cover Zffoto/Shutterstock.com; p. 5 SharonPhoto/Shutterstock.com; p. 6 Sergey Novikov/Shutterstock.com; p. 9 © iStockphoto.com/MattoMatteo; p. 10 Tyler Olson/Shutterstock.com; pp. 14, 24 (computer) © iStockphoto.com/3bugsmom; p. 17 © iStockphoto.com/JasonDoiy; pp. 18, 24 (library card) SW Productions/Photodisc/Getty Images; p. 21 Brenda Carson/Shutterstock.com; p. 22 wavebreakmedia/Shutterstock.com; p. 24 (computer) Hywit Dimyadi/Shutterstock.com.

Library of Congress Cataloging-in-Publication Data

Austen, Mary.
What do librarians do? / by Mary Austen.
p. cm. — (Helping the community)
Includes index.
ISBN 978-1-4994-0640-5 (pbk.)
ISBN 978-1-4994-0641-2 (6 pack)
ISBN 978-1-4994-0643-6 (library binding)
1. Librarians — Juvenile literature. 2. Libraries — Juvenile literature. I. Austen, Mary. II. Title.
Z682.A97 2016
020'.92—d23

Manufactured in the United States of America

CPSIA Compliance Information: Batch #WS15PK: For Further Information contact Rosen Publishing, New York, New York at 1-800-237-9932

CONTENTS

At the Library 4

Using Computers 15

A Library Card 16

Libraries Are Fun! 20

Words to Know 24

Index 24

Websites 24

A library is a place with many books.

You can borrow books
from the library.

You can borrow movies and music from the library, too.

A librarian is someone who works at a library.

Librarians help you find books. They also help you find movies and music.

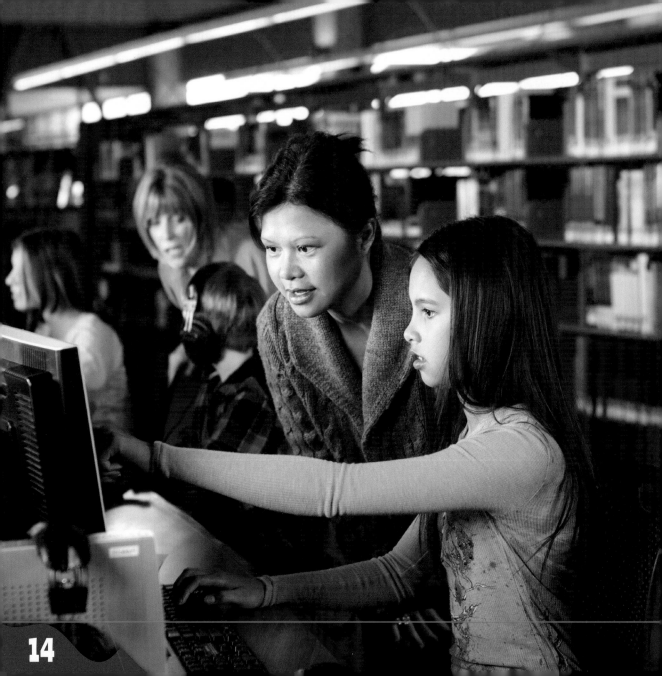

Libraries have **computers** for people to use. Librarians can help you use the computers.

Librarians also help you borrow things from the library.

First, you give the librarian your **library card**. Then, you can borrow things.

You can also do activities at the library. You can make crafts there!

Librarians help make the library a fun place to visit!

WORDS TO KNOW

computer

library card

INDEX

A
activities, 20

C
computers, 15

B
books, 4, 7, 12

L
library card, 19

WEBSITES

Due to the changing nature of Internet links, PowerKids Press has developed an online list of websites related to the subject of this book. This site is updated regularly. Please use this link to access the list: www.powerkidslinks.com/htc/lib